Eco-Buddhism
Caring for the Earth with Compassion

Table of Contents

Chapter 1. Introduction

Dive into an enlightening journey of compassion and environmental consciousness with our Special Report, "Eco-Buddhism: Caring for the Earth with Compassion." This accessible read will immerse you in a profound understanding of how ancient Buddhist spiritual principles and modern ecological awareness intersect, leading to transformative actions for our beloved Planet. Unveiling both the external environment's intricate beauty and the serenity found within our inner selves, you'll be inspired to make a harmonic shift reflective of your relationship with the Earth. Embark on this enriching odyssey, deepen your understanding of our interconnected world, and discover how you can compassionately contribute to the preservation of the globe. Your voyage into Eco-Buddhism awaits, illuminating your path one mindful step at a time.

Chapter 2. Discovering Eco-Buddhism: An Introduction

Modern humanity stands at a crucial juncture, facing perilous challenges that demand a fundamental transformation in our attitudes about the preservation and sanctity of our world. These profound shifts necessitate a new understanding of our connections with nature, facilitating a compassionate response to the ongoing ecological crisis.

2.1. Transitional Reverence: Bridging Religiosity and Ecology

Buddhism and ecology have shared a deep and intricate relationship since the emergence of the spiritual tradition around 2,500 years ago. The teachings of the Buddha emphasize interconnectedness and mutual dependence, doctrines which resonate abundantly with contemporary ecological understanding. Buddhism does not view humans as separate entities from the natural world; rather, it considers humanity an integral component of the interconnected web of life, thereby guiding adherents to a lifestyle that minimally impacts the environment.

By cultivating a sense of respect for nature, Buddhism fosters a non-exploitative relationship between humans and the Earth. This approach mirrors modern ecological movements, infusing spirituality into sustainability, resulting in a religiously-based ecological consciousness.

2.2. Kernel of Eco-Buddhism: Interconnectedness

Interconnectedness, known as pratītyasamutpāda in the Buddhist doctrine, connotes that every existence arises from a cause and, in turn, contributes to the generation of others. In this animated web of life, every element holds an essential position, contributing to the dynamism of the whole. This concept profoundly reciprocates with ecological viewpoints, emphasizing an intimate and reciprocal relationship between various environmental factors and species, with humanity as just one strand in the tapestry.

Recognizing this interconnected existence compels one to acknowledge that any harm inflicted upon nature rebounds upon humans, and vice versa. This realization can trigger an ethical transformation, relegating harmful attitudes to the margins and putting forth compassionate action as the cornerstone of our interactions with the Earth.

2.3. Mindfulness and Ecological Consciousness

Mindfulness, another important concept in Buddhism, implies being fully present in the moment, in tune with one's surroundings, perceiving them without being clouded by judgement or distortion. This comprehensive awareness drives one to see things as they truly are, accepting the reality of impermanence and the consequences of one's actions.

Seamlessly integrating mindfulness with an environmental perspective, individuals can observe the state of the world uncompromisingly, free from the misleading glamour of materialistic distractions. This clear vision illuminates the repercussions of harmful human activities on the planet, engendering a sense of ecological responsibility and the need for effective amendment.

2.4. Mettā (Loving Kindness) and Karunā (Compassion): Spiritual Anchors for Environmental Activism

Mettā and Karunā are deeply cherished values in Buddhism. Mettā encourages benevolence, goodwill, and loving-kindness towards all; Karunā underlines empathy and compassion for the troubled. These virtues stimulate an effective response towards suffering, both in humans and nature. Through empathetic distress at the sight of environmental degradation, individuals become motivated to find remedies, asserting the sanctity inherent in every creature.

Aligning Mettā and Karunā with environmental consciousness, we transform our view from a passive 'caring about' nature, to an active 'caring for' nature, promoting engaged environmental activism. Practising these virtues, Eco-Buddhism propounds the idea of universal environmental stewardship.

2.5. The Path Forward

Buddhism's millennia-old teachings offer profound insights into establishing an ethical and religious ethos that cherishes the environment. Through these teachings, we can conceptualize and give rise to Eco-Buddhism, a kind of spiritual environmentalism tethered to compassion. This path cultivates sensitivity to the environment's intricate life systems, fostering a conscientious and caring alliance with nature.

Among the billions of individuals on Earth, each can take upon themselves the duty of a karmic custodian, cherishing our shared planet – not as tacit entitlement or soulless property, but as a precious blessing reverberating with life and wisdom.

The first step on this Earth-friendly journey is to accept and internalize the fundamental truth of our interconnectedness with all forms of life, setting the stage for an ecological revolution anchored in wisdom and compassion. Let's make a collective stride towards a compassionate and sustainable world – because when it comes to the environment, it is not just about us; it is about all beings inhabiting this shared space we call home. This is the heart of Eco-Buddhism, the spiritual call for an environmental awakening.

Chapter 3. Buddhist Principles: The Pathway to Conscious Living

In the majestic realm of Buddhist thought, two key principles serve as the core. These elements provide a guiding light as we traverse the path of conscious living with the environment in mind. These principles are the Four Noble Truths and the Noble Eightfold Path.

3.1. The Four Noble Truths: Understanding Suffering

The first foundational concept to grasp in Buddhism is the Four Noble Truths. They serve as a framework for understanding human suffering and how to alleviate it.

The cornerstone of the Four Noble Truths is dukkha, usually translated as 'suffering' or 'unsatisfactoriness.' However, the term is more nuanced, expressing the fundamental discomfort we experience when living out of sync with our natural environment and our true nature. We often struggle against this insidious pain, driven by ignorance of its root causes.

The second truth is the origin of dukkha or suffering, referred to as samudaya. This encompassing root, according to Buddhism, is clinging or desire (taṇhā). This craving extends to every domain of our lives, including material goods, experiences, and ideologies. When we grasp onto these things as being innately satisfying or necessary for happiness, we establish patterns of craving and aversion, leading to ecological harm.

Next, we arrive at the cessation of dukkha, known as nirodha. Here,

Buddhism states that it is possible to end suffering by relinquishing clinging and ignorance. This indicates not only the potential for personal liberation but also environmental remediation.

The fourth Noble Truth is magga, which sets forth the path to the cessation of suffering. This path is a guide to living in alignment with reality as it is, free of ignorance and clinging—it's the Noble Eightfold Path.

3.2. The Noble Eightfold Path: Reframing Our Existence

The Noble Eightfold Path—right view, right intention, right speech, right action, right livelihood, right effort, right mindfulness, and right concentration—provides a blueprint on how to live consciously with regards to oneself, others, and the environment.

The right view signifies understanding the Four Noble Truths, the impermanent nature of reality, and the interconnectedness of all beings. It is through this view that we can appreciate the intricate ecosystems that govern our planet and recognize the consequences of our actions on the environment.

Right intention demands a commitment to act out of kindness, empathy, and compassion. Applying this to environmental consciousness, we then treat our surroundings with respect, not as a resource to exploit, but as a shared home to nurture.

Right speech is about truthful, beneficial, and non-harming communication. In the context of environmental responsibility, it encompasses speaking against unjust practices harming our planet, promoting sustainable living, and educating others about environmental issues.

Right action regards observing ethical conduct or, in Buddhist terms, the five precepts. These involve abstaining from killing living beings, stealing, sexual misconduct, lying, and intoxication. Ecologically, this means reducing harm by conscious consumption, promoting biodiversity, and opposing practices that exploit or harm the environment.

Right livelihood concerns making a living through ethical means. Those committed to conscious living can strive for careers that contribute positively to the environment, limit wastage, and support sustainability.

Right effort relates to our willful commitment to cultivate positive states of mind and alleviate harmful ones. This could mean fostering an appreciation for nature's beauty, which, in turn, fuels our motivation to protect the environment.

Right mindfulness develops an acute awareness and attention to our body, feelings, mind, and objects. By being present and mindful, we can tread lightly on the earth, leading to a reduction of our ecological footprint.

Finally, right concentration invites us to refine our capacity for focus, usually developed through meditative practices. Here, we learn to single-mindedly invest our energies into the preservation and respect of our world.

3.3. Buddhism & Environmentalism: A Symbiosis

The Noble Eightfold Path serves as a profound guide for the journey toward harmony with the environment. It illuminates the notion that personal well-being and the well-being of our planet are intrinsically intertwined. In essence, by aligning ourselves with these principles, we can advance towards an ecologically conscious form of spirituality that bridges the divide between self and nature.

Buddhist principles, therefore, breathe life into the concept of environmental consciousness. The interdependent nature of reality, central to Buddhist philosophy, validates the ecological principle of connectedness in the biosphere. In essence, if we harm our Earth, we harm ourselves. Conversely, when we care for it, we nurture our own lives too.

By understanding the depths of these Buddhist teachings, we can navigate the bustling modern world with wisdom, empathy, and ecological conscientiousness. Every step along this path is an affirmation of our love for the Earth, fostering a world where we preserve the environment not out of obligation, but out of deep respect and compassion.

Thus, Buddhism doesn't merely offer a set of abstract teachings on life and suffering; it provides practical strategies to cultivate a mind and heart that respects all life forms, leading the way towards conscious living and environmental preservation. It is a journey that demands courage, dedication, and above all, mindfulness. When adopted, it lampoons an individual's transformation into an Eco-Buddhist, translating their love for the environment into impactful change.

Chapter 4. The Five Precepts: Their Environmental Implications

At the heart of Buddhist ethical conduct lie the Five Precepts, a set of guidelines urging individuals to refrain from harmful actions and embrace virtues that foster peace, respect and compassion. While these precepts are primarily expressed as directives for personal behavior, amidst the unfolding environmental crisis, they acquire a critical relevance for ecological actions. Each precept, in its essence, carries environmental implications that, when mindfully integrated, can have profound impacts on our attitude towards the planet and its beings.

4.1. The First Precept: Abstaining from Killing

The first precept urges us to refrain from intentionally killing any living being. In a direct sense, this precept has always promoted vegetarianism among Buddhists, owing to its apparent call for nonviolence towards all animal life. The implications transcend dietary habits, suggesting a broader attitude of respect towards all forms of life, paralleling the fundamental pillars of ecological behavior.

However, an environmentally conscious interpretation requires an expansion of thought: Considering the carbon footprints, resource consumption, deforestation, soil degradation, water pollution, and massive biodiversity loss associated with industrial animal farming, it becomes clear that our dietary choices extend far beyond the plate in front of us, and are deeply entwined with the wellbeing of the planet.

Additionally, this precept guides us to refrain from actions directly causing harm to the environment, such as deforestation, pollution, and excessive consumerism. When drawn into the ecological fold, the first precept becomes a call to minimise harm to ecosystems and to live harmoniously with all forms of life, upholding biodiversity and ecological integrity as non-negotiable facets of ethical conduct.

4.2. The Second Precept: Abstaining from Stealing

The second precept prohibits taking that which is not freely given. In an environmental context, this translates to refraining from exploiting nature's resources unfairly or excessively.

Today, natural resources are rapidly depleting due to overconsumption, driven by lifestyles of excess and a prevalent culture of disposability. A mindful application of the second precept would encourage us to question our consumption patterns, promoting minimalism, conscious consumerism, and refusing, reducing, reusing, and recycling as integral facets of our lifestyle. It reminds us that the Earth's resources are finite, valuable, and to be shared among all beings, present and future.

Also, this precept reinforces the environmental justice movement's call to respect indigenous land rights and protect marginalized communities against exploitation. It is an ethical obligation to prevent theft of lands, resources, and livelihoods from those who have lived in harmonious connection with the Earth for generations.

4.3. The Third Precept: Abstaining from Sexual Misconduct

In its original form, the third precept addresses sexual misconduct, guiding individuals towards respectful and consensual relationships.

When contemplated through an ecological lens - it reflects respect for the relationship we have with Mother Earth. It mandates gentle interaction, reverence and maintaining pure, uncorrupted relationships with the environment around us. The principle of consent transforms into taking only with nature's permission, and "infidelity" translates to betrayal of our environmental responsibilities.

A more tangible reading could involve the understanding of how our decisions, particularly involving reproduction, hold environmental implications. It calls for mindfulness about our planetary footprint, conscious of the impact future generations will exert on the world's resources.

4.4. The Fourth Precept: Abstaining from False Speech

The fourth precept, at first glance, appears least relevant to environmental actions, but it is extremely critical. Committing to honesty and transparent communication is the bedrock of effective environmental advocacy. Misinformation, denial, and dissimulation have clouded the public understanding of the anthropogenic climate crisis. Upholding truth is fundamental to directing individual and collective actions that can address these environmental challenges.

This precept stresses on telling the ecological truth about the severity of the crisis, the urgent need for transformative change, and the consequences of inaction. This commitment extends to holding corporations and governments accountable for environmental degradation, demanding transparency and honesty, and challenging greenwashing.

4.5. The Fifth Precept: Abstaining from Intoxicants

The fifth precept, traditionally viewed as an prohibition against intoxicating substances that cloud the mind, has a direct ecological dimension. It promotes a conscious avoidance of activities that might muddy our relationship with the natural world or result in its degradation.

Indirectly, it advises us to steer clear of the intoxication of consumerism, the relentless pursuit of material possessions, and the illusion of happiness associated with acquisition and consumption. Recognizing and challenging this intoxication could lead to a mental shift towards simplicity, sustainability, and a holistic sense of wellbeing.

Echoing the ideals of mindfulness and conscious living, it advocates for a lifestyle that keeps our mental and physical environment clean, promoting not only personal health, but also the health of our planet.

In conclusion, the Five Precepts, when contemplated with an ecological consciousness, become powerful tools in nurturing a sustainable and compassionate relationship with our planet. They remind us of the intimate connection between personal ethics and environmental health, encouraging us to integrate these values in our everyday decisions, and foster a way of being that sympathetically resonates with the Earth's rhythm. With every mindful step we take, we move closer to becoming environmental Bodhisattvas, upholding the welfare of all sentient beings, and walking the path of Eco-Buddhism with steadfast dedication.

Chapter 5. Interconnectedness: Unveiling the Eco in Buddhism

In the heart of Buddhism, we discover the concept of "Pratitya-samutpada," or interconnectedness, implying that all phenomena are interconnected and interdependent. This theme, deeply etched into the spiritual lore of Buddhism, finds a striking resonance with modern ecology's principles, creating a sublime fusion referred to as Eco-Buddhism.

5.1. Manifestation of Interconnectedness in Buddhism

Buddhist philosophy maintains that all phenomena are without an absolute or independent existence, interdependently originating in reliance upon each other. This sacred understanding can be traced back to the teachings of the Buddha, who emphasized the deep connections amongst beings. Buddha's earliest discourses outline the doctrine of the Twelve Nidanas or twelve interdependent causes and effects that give rise to the cycle of existence.

Reflect upon the Lotus Sutra, a key text of Mahayana Buddhism, where the Buddha uses the visual metaphor of Indra's net to explain interconnectedness. Envision the Universe as an infinite net with multiple nodes where every node represents a phenomenon. At each node exists a gem reflecting all other nodes, signifying that each phenomenon is, in itself, the totality of existence.

5.2. Buddhism and Ecology: Marrying the Ancient and Modern

Modern ecology's principles align perfectly with the ancient wisdom of Buddhism, despite being separated by centuries in thought and origin. Ecology stresses the importance of interrelationships, drawing emphasis on ecosystems and the delicate balance that supports life. From such a perspective, no organism or entity lives in isolation. The health of an entire ecosystem depends upon each organism playing its part, thus validating interconnectedness.

The Gaia hypothesis, proposed by James Lovelock, imagines Earth as a superorganism, suggesting that all parts work together to maintain conditions ideal for life. This echoes the teachings of Buddhism, promoting the undivided unity of all phenomenon, the inseparable yoking of all life forms—a harmony amongst humans, animals, and the Earth.

5.3. Shambhala Principle and Enlightened Society

The realm of Shambhala, a legendary kingdom described in olden texts, signifies a space of spiritual tranquility, manifesting enlightened society. Shambhala Principle, advanced by Chögyam Trungpa, recognizes the basic goodness in all, resonating with the logic of interconnectedness. By presenting an enlightened society, we understand that human actions can either foster well-being of the Earth or lead to its destruction.

The Shambhala Principle cautions us about self-centeredness, reminding us of the need to acknowledge our interconnection with nature, and the inherent responsibility it carries. This shift in worldview, from self to all-encompassing, invokes us to tread lightly on the Earth, fostering a benevolent relationship with nature.

5.4. Madhyamaka View and Deep Ecology

Deep ecology, a radical environmental philosophy developed by Norwegian philosopher Arne Naess, involves authentic self-realization that recognizes humankind as part of the larger Earth, encouraging profound respect for all life forms. This aligns seamlessly with the Madhyamaka view in Buddhism, which talks of the 'Emptiness' or 'Sunyata', challenging the notion of standalone existence of phenomena in favor of relational existence.

The alignment of deep ecology and the Madhyamaka view opens up paths to a more enlightened form of ecological stewardship. On realizing that we are just one part of a vast, interconnected system, we're naturally inclined to dispose of harmful, unsustainable practices, nurturing our planet proactively.

5.5. Practical Interconnectedness: Community Sustainability

Addressing the abstract theory of interconnectedness in Buddhism and modern ecology is valuable. However, it is also necessary to affirm how an understanding of this principle molds environmentally conscious actions in individual lives and communities.

These actions include a lifestyle of mindfulness and consciousness of one's choices—conserving resources, advocating for animal rights, supporting organic farming, composting and reducing waste—a way of life that aligns with the ethics of 'right livelihood' in Buddhism.

Asia's tradition of 'Forest Monks,' is another example, who base their practice on dwelling mindfully in nature, protecting forests, advocating sustainable harvesting, a testament to practical interconnectedness.

In conclusion, the concept of interconnectedness lies at the heart of Buddhism and modern ecology, serving as the connective tissue between spiritual practice and environmental actions. Along with recognizing our symbiosis with nature, Eco-Buddhism also advocates an enlightened eco-consciousness, prompting us to redefine our relationship with the Earth, fostering compassionate care for our shared planet.

Chapter 6. Mindfulness and Sustainability: Treading Lightly on Earth

Speaking of mindfulness in terms of Buddhism immediately brings to mind the teachings of Thich Nhat Hanh, a beloved Zen master and a protege of global mindfulness practice. Thich Nhat Hanh emphasizes the "oneness" of humans and nature, a recognition that can bridge the gap between ourselves and the environment, broadening the scope of our compassion to include all life. Mindfulness, a key principal in Buddhist teachings, urges us to become profoundly aware of our immediate experiences. When applied to our relationship with the Earth, mindfulness can evoke a profound shift in attitudes and habits that might be damaging to our world. This intimate understanding leads to considered, conscious decisions culminating in sustainability.

6.1. The Zen of Environmental Awareness

To initiate the journey toward environmental mindfulness, it's essential to understand how deeply connected we are to nature. Thich Nhat Hanh calls this "interbeing," the understanding that we inter-are with everything else in the universe. A flower, for instance, is not solely a flower—it consists of sunlight, soil, time, space, rain, and the gardener's efforts. Similarly, our existence is the amalgamation of countless components, from the air we breathe to the food we consume. Acknowledging this interconnectedness is the first significant step toward environmental mindfulness.

6.2. Practicing Mindfulness

Mindfulness can be practiced in multiple ways but principally focuses on the cultivation of presence. Here, simple activities such as washing our hands, taking a walk, or eating can transform into opportunities for deep ecological reflections. Consider taking a walk in the park. Each footfall can remind us of our physical connection with the Earth. The rustling leaves, the stones beneath our shoes, the breath of wind on our faces, are all reminders of the Earth's ceaseless giving. Such mindful walks infuse us with gratitude and awareness of our dependence on nature.

6.3. Mindful Consumption

Closely tied with practicing mindfulness is conscious consumption. Sentient creatures that we are, we consume to exist, but mindfulness calls for moderation and thoughtfulness. This translates to adopting a sustainable lifestyle—reducing waste, reusing items, choosing public transportation, opting for goods produced sustainably—that minimizes harm to our planet. Mindful consumption is not about thriving with less; instead, it concerns the understanding and acknowledging how our choices affect the Earth and its other inhabitants.

6.4. Embracing Simplicity

Simplicity underpins mindfulness. The primary principles of Buddhism—non-attachment and understanding the impermanence of things—guide us toward a less cluttered, simpler lifestyle. This might translate to reducing physical belongings, but it also extends to our emotional and mental domains. Regular periods of silence, reflection, or self-examination are integral to embracing simplicity. Both simplicity and sustainability are married in their shared goal of causing less harm and conserving, whether it be resources or peace of mind.

6.5. Compassion in Action

Mindfulness is not a dormant state of being. The Buddhisattva's life is one of compassionate action guided by wisdom. When consciously fostered, mindfulness blooms into compassion, both for ourselves and everything around us. Seen under the light of interbeing, rainforests are not just resources; they are fellow sentient beings. Similarly, air and water are not merely utilities but life-givers we need to respect and protect. Compassionate action for the environment grows when we broaden our notion of what constitutes a 'being,' extending our empathy towards all life.

6.6. The Interplay of Inner and Outer Ecology

A crucial aspect of mindfulness as a guiding principle of sustainable practices lies in its ability to reflect our inner ecology's state in the outer world. Our individual thoughts, beliefs, and practices cascade onto our surroundings, affecting the global milieu. The external environmental crisis rife with pollution, disparately distributed resources, and rapid biodiversity loss, thus reflects a profound inner crisis—an erosion of conscious awareness and connection. Returning to mindfulness, to an awareness of interbeing, can steer us toward sustainable solutions that respect and uphold nature's balance.

6.7. Cultivating an Ecosattva

An 'Ecosattva' is a new generation environmental warrior imbued with mindfulness. Cultivating an Ecosattva involves a deep commitment to mindful living, compassionate action, and the willingness to challenge current destructive norms. Contrary to common belief, an Ecosattva isn't a hermit living in the woods but a mindful individual consciously engaging with urban landscapes, becoming change agents within their own spheres. You and I could be Ecosattvas, warriors striving to protect and cherish our shared home.

In conclusion, mindfulness is a potent tool that imbues empathy and encourages ecological responsibility, playing a significant role in sustainable practices. Rooted in compassion, mindfulness and sustainability together can guide us in treading lightly on the Earth. Following these practices mindfully can allow us to align with Mother Nature, seeking refuge in her wisdom as we charter a sustainable path forward.

Chapter 7. Compassion in Action: The Role of Karuna in Eco-Buddhism

For centuries, Buddhist practitioners have cultivated compassion, also known as 'Karuna,' on their spiritual path. Within this extensive concept, one uncovers an imperative to the 'Eco-Buddhism' conversation - how compassion helps to uphold the wellness and survival of our planet, Earth.

7.1. The Concept of Karuna in Traditional Buddhism

Reputed as the "jewel in the crown" of Buddhist philosophy, Karuna or compassion is a fundamental teaching. It underlines the empathy one feels towards the suffering of others, alongside a deep yearning to alleviate their pain. The Buddha himself taught the cultivation of four 'immeasurables': loving kindness, compassion, empathetic joy, and equanimity. Among these, compassion is regarded as the catalyst to initiate tangible actions intended to lessen suffering.

The term 'Karuna' signifies 'to cry out.' It is the emotional response generated when confronted with the distress of others — a reverberation echoing their torment. If 'Metta,' or loving-kindness, observes one's happiness, then Karuna is its mirror image, addressing the palpable perils that bar wellbeing.

Contrary to short-lived emotional sentiment, Karuna should be understood as an enduring spiritual disposition. It is an attitude, rather than an emotional state, a call towards action inspired by the understanding of interconnected suffering.

7.2. Karuna and Interconnectedness: Embracing the Whole

A concept regularly discussed alongside Karuna is 'Pratityasamutpada' or 'Dependent Origination,' which accentuates the interconnectedness in Buddhism. It encapsulates the idea that everything exists relative to everything else. No entity, animate or inanimate, exists in isolation. All phenomena are interconnected, subject to a web of causes and conditions.

In this dense web of life, there is no room for a bystander. Every action has a subsequent reaction, rippling its effects across the network. Therefore, entering the worldly dance of dependent origination with deep understanding and compassion can lead to beneficial outcomes for all interconnected entities.

Comprehension of this profound interdependence deepens our sense of compassion. The suffering of fellow beings becomes our suffering, their joy, our joy. Acknowledging this bond with all life forms, we rediscover the urgency for compassionate action to ease collective suffering and contribute positively to our common home – Earth.

7.3. Compassion in Ecology: Karuna in the Face of Climate Crisis

Now more than ever, our planet is in a state of distress. Ecological destruction wrought by rampant consumerism, exploitation of resources, and neglect of natural habitats has pushed many species to the brink of extinction and brought about a climate crisis bearing severe penalties for all forms of life.

The application of Karuna seems indispensable amid the growing ecological emergency. Buddhism's compassionate approach offers a pathway for humans to reconsider their relationship with nature — not as dominators, but as its conscious inhabitants and caretakers.

Understanding the suffering of our ecosystems and the creatures inhabiting them requires a karuna-driven paradigm shift. One where we don't just perceive the Earth as an environment we live in but rather an interconnected entity to which we belong.

7.4. Karuna: A Call to Environmental Mindfulness and Action

Embracing Karuna invites a mindful response to the environmental calamities we've instigated, with our uncritical participation in environmentally detrimental systems. Compassion compels us to examine our actions' ecological implications and inspires more sustainable lifestyles.

For Buddhism, the alleviation of suffering incorporates environmental wellness. An environmentalist, acting from Karuna, works not just for self-preservation but acknowledges their role within the vast, interconnected global ecosystem. They bear the shared responsibility of co-creating a harmonious world.

Applying compassionate action in the eco-context translates to individual and collective efforts to reduce our carbon footprint. This might involve behaviour as simple as reducing, reusing, and recycling our waste, or as complex as advocating and implementing systemic changes that protect and preserve our ecosystems.

7.5. Harnessing the Power of Karuna in a Global Movement

With compassion at its core, Eco-Buddhism instigates a shift from myopic self-interest towards an ecocentric approach, emphasizing the importance of all beings sharing our planet. It encourages the active participation of all in a global call to environmental action.

Karuna reiterates the Buddhist ideal of interconnectedness, drives us towards acknowledging the plight we've imposed on our environment, and encourages steps towards remediation. The climate crisis beckons a compassionate response - one that aligns individual actions with global efforts to heal our world. By fostering a compassionate ethos, we are not just securing the planet's future but are simultaneously creating a loving, caring society.

In the face of climate change and environmental degradation, Karuna is not merely a Buddhist principle to be appreciated, but a calling for all humans to understand, cultivate, and manifest. It fosters a synergy of mindfulness, empathy, and sustainable action, capable of leading humanity towards more harmonious coexistence with the Earth.

Through Karuna, we may not only relieve our planet's sufferings but also touch the intrinsic interdependence and preciousness of all life. It is the heart of Eco-Buddhism, encouraging prudence, respect, and love for all entities co-inhabiting our common home, without which we cannot survive — let alone thrive.

Chapter 8. Learning from Thích Nhất Hạnh: Engaged Buddhism in Practice

Thích Nhất Hạnh, a globally revered Zen master, peace activist, and the founder of the Engaged Buddhism movement, offered a remarkable leg up to the complex relationship between Buddhism and environmental consciousness. His teachings, deeply rooted in Buddhist principles, have shown us the path toward deeper understanding, compassionate living, and profound respect for all life forms on Earth, guiding us to bridge the chasm between spirituality and environmentalism.

8.1. Embracing Interbeing

One of Nhất Hạnh's most significant teachings is the concept of Interbeing - a term he coined to represent the interconnectedness of all life. Defined as the understanding that we inter-are with every other entity in the universe, Interbeing is a concept that ties into quantum physics, ontology, and the Buddhist core principle of dependent co-arising.

Nothing exists in isolation; each form is empty of a separate existence yet full of everything else in the cosmos. Understanding this, one realizes that to care for one's self is to care for the world around them. Nhất Hạnh highlights this concept and consistently weaves it into his teachings on ecology and mindful living.

In his 2008 publication, "The World We Have: A Buddhist Approach to Peace and Ecology," Nhất Hạnh explains how the state of our planet is the physical manifestation of our actions, thoughts, and speech, influenced by the veil of ignorance over the principle of Interbeing. By reminding ourselves of this interconnectedness, we can inspire mindful actions benefitting the self, others, and the natural world.

8.2. Compassionate Consumption

Nhất Hạnh expanded the Five Mindfulness Trainings, a set of ethical guidelines in Buddhism, to include detailed teachings on conscious consumption. This fifth precept, initially dealing with the avoidance of intoxicants harmful to the mind and body, was extended to incorporate the concept of compassionate consumption.

He edifies that what we consume directly affects our well-being and the health of the planet. This encompasses not just what we eat, but also the media we consume, the products we purchase, and the energy we use. The practice of mindful consumption - being fully aware and present with the choices we make impacts our engagement with the world, allowing us to contribute to less harm and more healing.

8.3. A Call to Mindful Action

Nhất Hạnh's teachings exhort action from a place of deep mindfulness and compassion. Regarded as the father of Engaged Buddhism, he emphasizes the need to practice mindfulness both in meditation and in everyday life. This path encourages individuals to combine the inner work of mindfulness with the outer work of social and ecological action.

His teachings magnify the urgency of mindfulness in all forms of activism. For Nhất Hạnh, there isn't a division between having a spiritual life and living an engaged life. It's in the everyday actions, in gardening, washing dishes, or walking mindfully where we can engage with ourselves and the world with awareness. Engaged Buddhism in this sense is the culmination of a dialectic process, amalgamating personal peace with a sense of social justice and environmental responsibility.

8.4. Conclusion: Walking as if Kissing the Earth

Thích Nhất Hạnh has given humanity a compassionate and mindful approach to our relationship with the Earth. He typifies that we walk on this Earth not as separate beings, but as an intricate part of the interconnected web of existence, explaining, "We have to walk in a way that we only print peace and serenity on the Earth. Walk as if you are kissing the Earth with your feet."

His teachings call for a profound transformation in our perceptions and actions toward the Earth. His emphasis on interbeing, compassionate consumption, and mindful action can guide us through the crises we face today, whether individual or global. Through his life and works, he has extended an arm to humanity, an invitation to step onto the path of mindfulness, engaging every step with serenity, compassion, and environmental awareness. His wisdom, a beacon guiding us towards conscious living, fostering an intimate relationship with the Earth that bears the imprint of peace, understanding, and love in our every step.

Chapter 9. Eco-Buddhist Practices for Modern Life

Through the centuries, Buddhism has maintained an unwavering focus on equanimity, mindfulness, and respect for all living beings. These principles, combined with contemporary environmental concern, have given birth to Eco-Buddhism. Modern life seethes with challenges and unending distractions. Yet, the principles of Eco-Buddhism can ground us, helping us to respond mindfully and compassionately. Let us now explore these practices that encourage ecological awareness and compassion.

9.1. Mindfulness: The Path to Awareness

Buddhist teachings often emphasize mindfulness, the attentive and non-judgmental observance of the present moment. This practice can help us appreciate our awareness, embracing our interconnection with the Earth. Moreover, mindfulness roots us in the present, where change happens, and thus invites us to direct our conscious and conscientious efforts towards the environment.

Start your day with a 15-minute mindfulness session. Sit comfortably and focus on your breath, sensations in your body, thoughts, and emotions. As you practice, you will experience a growing clarity about your intrinsic connection with the world around you.

9.2. Loving-Kindness: The Well-Spring of Compassion

The Pali term "Metta" translates to a familiar English word: "love" or "loving-kindness". This profound Buddhist concept encourages benevolence towards all living things. Try practicing Metta meditation. Begin with cultivating loving-kindness for yourself. Gradually extend this kindness outward to loved ones, neutral individuals, those with whom you share differences, and, ultimately, all beings in the universe.

This practice helps foster a compassionate heart, essential for an ecologically conscious lifestyle. As you grow in compassion, you will naturally evolve into a person considering the environmental impact of every action.

9.3. Simplicity: Reducing Consumption

Buddhism teaches the Middle Way, a path of moderation that sidesteps excess. Embracing this principle in daily life leads to a lifestyle of reduced consumption and minimal waste. By consciously curtailing our wants, we can limit our ecological footprint.

In everyday life, work on minimizing the use of plastic and other non-biodegradable products. Opt for public transport whenever feasible, reducing carbon emissions. Simple steps like these reflect eco-Buddhist values and contribute meaningfully to environmental protection.

9.4. Community Engagement and Environmental Activism

Buddhism extols the virtue of "Sangha" - the community. Similarly, the ecological movement thrives on collective action. Together, we can create a larger impact on environmental issues.

With your mindfulness and compassion bolstered by Buddhist practices, participate in local environmental initiatives. Join cleanups, plant trees, or start a community garden. Remember, every action, however small, counts.

9.5. Insight Meditation and Deep Ecology

Insight, or Vipassana meditation, pushes us towards profound wisdom concerning our reality's interdependent nature. This reflective practice aligns with the principles of Deep Ecology, a philosophy that espouses inherent worth to all living beings.

Deep Ecology urges humans to acknowledge and respect this interconnectedness, advocating for Nature's protection. Use insights from Vipassana to recognize and honor your interconnectedness with the Earth. Make this recognition a cornerstone of your environmentally responsible actions.

9.6. The Five Precepts and Eco-Ethics

The Five Precepts form Buddhism's ethical foundation. They proscribe against killing, stealing, sexual misconduct, lying, and intoxicants. Viewed through an eco-Buddhist lens, these Precepts can inform an ethical approach to environmental stewardship.

Discourage harmful activities that threaten life on Earth, fostering respect for biodiversity. Speak up against irresponsible consumption and waste that rob future generations. Unmask unsustainable practices and promote truth and transparency in environmental matters. Encourage sober and conscious living, shunning mindless over-consumption.

The practices outlined above form a practical roadmap for the application of Eco-Buddhism in our modern lives. Most importantly, they pave the way for a sustainable, compassionate world where humanity and the environment co-exist harmoniously. Through mindfulness, loving-kindness, simplicity, community engagement, insight meditation, and adhering to an eco-ethical interpretation of the Five Precepts, we can indeed make a significant positive impact on our world's ecological future.

Remember, the journey of Eco-Buddhism is one where the walk reflects the talk. As you move forward with these practices in your life, remind yourself that every conscious step you take hasn't just shifted you, but the world around you as well. Allow Eco-Buddhism to illuminate your path, encouraging you to connect deeper with the Earth and to cherish the resplendent beauty that is our shared home.

Chapter 10. Community and Change: Building an Eco-Buddhist Society

The harmonic connection between individual and community, echoed in every Buddhist principle, fuels the ecological consciousness revolution. No transformation exists in isolation. By incorporating these ethical foundations into everyday living, communities could blossom into strikingly vibrant Eco-Buddhist societies.

10.1. Awakening Collective Environmental Consciousness

Noticing the rebirths of eco-sentiments across society is the first step on this path. Just observe how modern lifestyle trends sway towards sustainability. More eco-friendly products are becoming commonplace. Individuals are commemorating Earth Day with zeal comparable to national holidays. Countless organizations are sprouting, devoted to reducing carbon footprints and endorsing the use of renewable energy.

Still, awakening collective environmental consciousness remains a formidable task. Deep-seated habits need to change, and discarded beliefs must be unlearned. It requires the dissolution of the long-held view that human beings hold dominion over nature.

How do we usher society towards this enlightened state of mind? It all pivots on embracing the core tenets of Buddhism. These principles bring an exquisite clarity to the links between human action and environmental consequence.

10.2. Interconnectedness: The Heart of Eco-Buddhism

If there's a heartbeat to Eco-Buddhism, it undoubtedly pulsates with the rhythm of interconnectedness. Known as Pratityasamutpada, it is a teaching that everything in the universe is interconnected. Grasping at this notion of interdependence paints a clear image of a seamless symbiosis where human and natural spheres coexist harmoniously - a picture of our potential Eco-Buddhist society.

This concept extends to a collective understanding of our intricate global ecosystem. One seemingly small action can ripple across the globe, affecting countless life forms. This is easy to forget in our fast-paced, increasingly digitized society. But the truth anchors deeply: 'We are the earth, and the earth is us.' Every resource we consume, every waste we produce, shapes our collective existence.

10.3. Ethical Living: Compassion Over Consumption

Transforming this understanding into personal and collective action is the next crucial step towards building an Eco-Buddhist society. It brings us to Right Action or Samyag Karmanta in Buddhism - ethical conduct based on love and compassion.

From individual actions like mindful consumption, recycling, and reducing waste, to collective endeavors like community farming or supporting local eco-friendly businesses, ethical choices can amass into sizeable impacts. It's about cultivating compassionate habits that mirror our staunch respect towards planet Earth.

10.4. Community Changes: Eco-Dharma

Bringing about community transformation draws from the Buddhist practice of Sangha, indicating community or collective practice. However, applying this in the context of our ecological crisis, we find a concept known as 'Eco-Dharma' - the fusion of ecological responsibility and holistic Buddhist practice.

Just as how the five ethical precepts in Buddhism guide individual behavior, communities can create sets of ecological principles or 'Green Precepts.' These could inspire eco-centric activities such as shared renewable energy projects, permaculture gardens, or community-supported agriculture.

10.5. Transitioning Towards Eco-Buddhist Societies: A Call to Action

The journey towards an Eco-Buddhist society will not be without hardship. Systemic issues like rampant consumerism, over-consumption, and socioeconomic inequality intersect with our environmental crisis. However, through Buddhist philosophy, communities worldwide have the potential to make steps necessary for this substantial shift, embodying the principles of interconnectedness, compassion, and mindful living.

Highlight the importance of education as a pillar for this transition. Promote awareness about the ecological crisis and our role within it. Employ Buddhist teachings to cultivate a deeper sense of compassion and respect for life in all its forms. Above all, through individual and collective effort, we can manifest this harmonious convergence of sustainability, spirituality, and society - the noble Eco-Buddhist society.

10.6. Concluding Thoughts

An Eco-Buddhist society is not an unattainable dream but a tangible reality achievable through collective commitment. An embodiment of the compassionate values taught in Buddhism and the ecological concerns of our time, it serves as an ultimate testament to human potential. Herein lies the promise of Eco-Buddhism, a journey that every sentient being can partake in, for the well-being of all life on the planet.

Chapter 11. Towards a Brighter Future: Applying Eco-Buddhist Wisdom for Environmental Stewardship

The dedication to a more sustainable and mindful approach towards our planet does not merely hinge on the external actions we take but is also deeply intertwined with our internal landscapes. By embracing the wisdom of Eco-Buddhism, we open ourselves to enduring lessons in environmental conservation and stewardship. Using simple, yet profound practices, we can evolve our outlook and inspire change that resonates on a global level.

11.1. Buddhist Principles and the Environment: A Harmonious Union

Tucked within the expansive teachings of Buddhism lie keys to cultivate a more mindful relationship with our environment. Fundamental Buddhist concepts such as the Four Noble Truths and the Eightfold Path provide a supportive framework for Earth-conscious living.

The First Noble Truth, acknowledging suffering (Dukkha), beholds the reality of environmental crises, from climate change to biodiversity loss. The Second Truth, understanding the cause of suffering (Samudaya), points to human actions—in overconsumption, pollution, and ignorant dealings with nature—as primary drivers of ecological destruction. The Third Truth, ceasing the cause of suffering (Nirodha), calls for radical changes in our treatment of nature. Lastly, the Fourth Noble Truth, the path leading to the cessation of suffering (Magga), provides a direction by endorsing right view, intention, speech, action, livelihood, effort, mindfulness, and concentration.

11.2. The Notion of Interconnectedness: Buddhist Ecology in Practice

Emphasizing on Anatta (no self) and Dependent Origination (interconnectedness of all phenomena), Buddhism inspires a deep ecological perspective, where humans are not separate entities, but part of the larger whole of nature.

In Buddhist ecology, elements like water, earth, fire (energy), and air are esteemed as respected entities, not mere resources. Recognizing our coexistence, we are led to reevaluate our dominant role and adopt a more harmonious interaction with nature.

11.3. Compassion and Loving-Kindness: Personal Values, Global Impact

The practices of Metta (loving-kindness) and Karuna (compassion), extend beyond human relationships to all sentient beings, further encompassing the entire living world. Reflecting these values in everyday actions contributes to a more sustainable and compassionate world.

Mindfulness, a central practice in Buddhism, cultivates our awareness of environmental impacts of our everyday choices—from consumption habits to waste generation. Mindful living nudges us to tread more gently on Earth, consume responsibly, and minimize waste, thereby reducing our carbon footprints.

11.4. Embracing Simplicity and Contentment: Towards Sustainable Living

Living in accordance with the concept of 'Santutthi' or contentment remarkably contributes to the sustainability of the planet. Fostering a sense of contentment and sufficiency opposes the modern consumerist culture that often leads to environmental degradation.

Simplicity in Buddhism, implied by mere satisfactions of basic needs, goes hand in hand with the principles of a circular economy—where decrease in consumption, reuse, recycle, and repairing becomes the norm.

11.5. The Power of Collective Responsibility: Buddhist Sanghas and Environmental Advocacy

Buddhist Sanghas or communities around the world are taking up the mantle of environmental stewardship. These communities' assertive actions, such as tree ordination in Thailand or anti-nuclear protests in Japan, underscore the constructive contribution religion can make in addressing environmental issues.

11.6. From Knowledge to Action: Practical Steps towards a Sustainable Future

As followers of the Buddha's path, we are encouraged to translate these profound insights into practical actions.

- Adopting eco-friendly lifestyles by reducing, reusing, and recycling our resources.

- Cultivating mindfulness of our consumption patterns to minimize environmental impact.

- Participating in or supporting initiatives that aim to protect and conserve the environment.

- Encouraging ethical investments that support sustainable development.

- Advocating for policies that address the crucial environmental challenges of our time.

Beyond just a personal commitment, environmental stewardship is an act of deep compassion for all beings and the planet. With Eco-Buddhism at the helm, we are urged to foster an ethos of responsibility, initiating a ripple-effect of positive change—an embodied wisdom that brings forth a brighter future for all. Eco-Buddhism asks us not just to behave responsibly, but also to shift the very grounds of our being, realizing our deep interconnection with the Earth and each other, and how the health of one affects the health of all. The journey towards Eco-Buddhism continues, inviting us to step forth and participate fully in caring for the Earth with compassion.